THE SERMONS OF
ST. FRANCIS DE SALES

ON

PRAYER

St. Francis de Sales
1567-1622
Bishop, Founder of the Visitation,
and Doctor of the Church

THE SERMONS OF
ST. FRANCIS DE SALES
ON
PRAYER

Translated by Nuns of the Visitation

Edited by Father Lewis S. Fiorelli, O.S.F.S.

Prayer is so useful and necessary that without it we could not come to any good, seeing that by means of prayer we are shown how to perform all our actions well.
—St. Francis de Sales

TAN BOOKS AND PUBLISHERS, INC.
Rockford, Illinois 61105

Nihil Obstat: Rev. Msgr. John H. Dewson
                  Censor Librorum

Imprimatur: Rev. Msgr. Paul J. Taggart
                  Administrator of the Diocese
                  Wilmington, Delaware
                  October 19, 1984

Copyright © 1985 by the Visitation Monastery of Frederick, MD, Inc.

Library of Congress Catalog Card Number: 84:52310

ISBN: 0-89555-258-2

Further volumes in preparation.

Printed and bound in the United States of America.

TAN BOOKS AND PUBLISHERS, INC.
P.O. Box 424
Rockford, Illinois 61105

1985

To the Most Holy Trinity
Who Created All Things for the Sake of Prayer

(From "The Goal of Prayer").

TABLE OF CONTENTS

ABOUT ST. FRANCIS DE SALES

St. Francis de Sales, the holy bishop, founder, and Doctor of the Church, is known throughout the Church for his great sanctity, learning, theological knowledge, gentleness, and understanding of the human soul. Through these marvelous gifts he converted and guided innumerable souls to God during his own lifetime, and re-converted thousands from Calvinism. He continues to direct many souls through his spiritual writings and published sermons. Today St. Francis de Sales is known as one of the great figures of the Catholic Counter-Reformation and of the 17th-century rebirth of Catholic mystical life.

St. Francis was born in 1567 in the castle belonging to the de Sales family in Thorens, Savoy, located in what is now southeastern France. As he grew older, the young nobleman studied literature, law, philosophy and theology in Paris and Padua, and received a doctorate in civil and canon law. Though he could have had a brilliant secular career, he set his heart on following God's call to the priesthood, and was ordained in 1593 at the age of 26. He was consecrated Bishop of Geneva at age 35, and remained the Bishop of Geneva for the remaining 20 years of his life.

Shortly after becoming a bishop, St. Francis met St. Jane Frances de Chantal, a widow; between these two saints there grew a deep spiritual friendship. St. Francis became the spiritual director of Jane Frances, and with her, he founded the religious order of nuns known as the Order of the Visitation, or the Visitandines.

St. Francis de Sales wrote two of the greatest Catholic masterpieces on the spiritual life: the *Introduction to the Devout Life* and *Treatise on the Love of God*. The former shows how holiness is possible for all people in the state of grace, including people living in the world. This book was a bestseller in the 17th century and is still popular today. The *Treatise on the Love of God* covers all aspects of the virtue of charity, the supernatural love of God. Because of his writings, St. Francis de Sales has become the patron of writers and journalists.

St. Francis de Sales died at age 55, in the year 1622. He was canonized in 1665, and was declared a Doctor of the Universal Church by Pope Pius IX in 1877. With this declaration the Church presented the teachings of St. Francis de Sales to all the faithful as a most sure guide to true Catholic doctrine and to the ways of the spiritual life—a most sure guide to Heaven.

PREFACE

A Benedictine recently published an article entitled, "Deux âmes fraternelles: S. Bernard et S. François de Sales"—"Two Brothers in the Spirit: St. Bernard and St. Francis de Sales." Very true! A Cistercian feels very much "at home" in listening to St. Francis. But so, I believe, will any Christian and lover of Christ.

These sermons not only begin by evoking the name of the great Abbot of Clairvaux, but have much of his style and flavor. There is the rich allegorical use of the Song of Songs in three of the sermons, and indeed of all parts of Scripture. There is hardly a line that does not contain at least a scriptural allusion. They evoke a whole array of scriptural types: Jacob, Tobit, Job, David, John the Baptist, and Paul.

At the same time St. Francis de Sales is a man of Tradition, drawing from the richness of Tradition. He uses the most ancient sources, the Fathers of the Desert, Sts. Antony and Paul; then Fathers from East and West, Sts. Gregory Nazianzen, Augustine and Jerome; as well as "The Last of the Fathers," St. Bernard of Clairvaux, and his contemporary, St. Bruno. The Franciscans are here, too: St. Francis of Assisi, Blessed Giles and St. Bonaventure; and the Dominican tradition in St. Catherine of Siena.

Yet Francis de Sales is a man of his times—the age of scholasticism. Even if, right at the beginning of his treatment of his topic, he does bring in the age-old paradigm of *lectio, meditatio, oratio* and *contemplatio,* his main approach is to study his subject through its causes: the final cause, the most important one, first; then the efficient, material and formal causes. Distinctions abound: There are three kinds of prayer, and three kinds of vocal prayer, and three kinds of sinners; four levels of prayer and four parts of mental prayer. Seeming contradictions of the Fathers are reconciled by careful distinctions, and carefully wrought syllogisms prove that neither God the Father nor Jesus, His Son, pray. Yet all this theology is never heavily labored. The rich patristic tradition with all its biblical imagery is so enfolded into it, as are St. Francis' own delightful images, that at times it cannot but evoke a smile. As a monk, I must confess I never imagined myself a pretty little bird held in the cage of the monastery to delight my Lord and King!

These sermons are well chosen for an introduction to St. Francis de Sales. They are very representative of the richness of his style. And they treat of what he himself declares to be at the heart of all his teaching: "Prayer is so useful and necessary that without it we could not come to any good." At the same time, these sermons are immediately useful for our everyday life. Francis gives us some clear understanding of the stages of growth in prayer, while still warning against getting caught up in a quest to "locate" ourselves on the journey. He has a few lucid remarks on the importance of posture and symbol, and very practical ideas on preparation for prayer, the use of ejaculations, and praying the Our Father. Most important, he reminds us that we go to prayer not to be good pray-ers or to enjoy the consolations of prayer; we go to prayer to find God and be united to Him. Seek the God of consolation and not the consolations of God. His teaching on prayer is clear, concise, and practical, and yet sublime. It goes all the way, deftly handling the graces of contemplation and the exquisite purification of all the interior faculties—while the apex of the spirit clings to God, beginning "here below what we shall do eternally in Heaven."

No matter where one is in the life of prayer, these sermons can be read again and again with immense profit and fruit. We can be grateful to Father Lewis Fiorelli and to TAN Books and Publishers for making them readily available to us in English.

Father M. Basil Pennington, O.C.S.O.

TRANSLATOR'S NOTE

The four sermons on prayer contained in this book were translated from St. Francis de Sales' *Oeuvres,* vol. IX (Annecy: Niérat, 1892-1964), pp. 46-72. The Introduction entitled "Origins of the Sermons" is an excerpt from the foreword to the Annecy edition (pages v-x and xviii-xix). For the most part, the only references given here are Scriptural references. (When giving his sermons, St. Francis de Sales often paraphrased the Scriptures.) Those interested in more scholarly use of these sermons may wish to consult the Annecy edition for classical and patristic references.

INTRODUCTION

Origins of the Sermons

The sermons of St. Francis de Sales are divided into two series: those signed and those received. This division is based not only on the mode of transmission by which they have come down to us, but also upon the special character, even the very nature, of these sermons. Some have been preserved for us just as they left the pen of the orator; others, just as they fell from his lips, or at least just as they had been heard and understood by his hearer. Each of these two series has its special merit, its proper form, its determined shape. In the first, one discovers the light and lively thought of the author and sees delineated the logic of his deductions, the force of his arguments. In the second, one notices particularly the charms of his gracious and imaginative word. In both, his intelligence and his heart are revealed.

What we have just said concerns only form, but an essential difference distinguishes these two classes of sermons. The signed sermons, which for the most part had been delivered before a large public group, reveal the major lines of formal discourse; they are replete with erudition, strewn with texts from Sacred Scripture and with practical applications appropriate to the most varied situations. All the subjects of doctrine and morals, indeed even a number of points of controversy, are treated or touched upon in these sermons. This is not the case with the received sermons, which are addressed principally to a particular audience, subjected to special obligations of which the preacher never loses sight. Here he applies himself more to touching souls than to instruction. It is the language of a father much more than that of a master or a pastor.

Under the rubric of "received sermons" must be included the talks given at the Chapel of the Visitation, which were written and carefully preserved by the religious who heard them. It was a precious manna which the daughters of this saintly bishop gathered up; but unlike the Israelites who put nothing aside for the next day, these sisters made provisions for the future of their institute, and even for the edification of the entire Christian people. Besides, they had had precedents in their labor. During the Lenten stations preached at Dijon and later at Grenoble, and in still other cities, St. Francis de Sales had seen men of the first rank stationed assiduously at the foot of his chair in order to write down his admirable instructions as delivered. Unfortunately these collections, which might have been of such great value for posterity, are lost today. We must be content with those which the Sisters of the Visitation have preserved for us.

Remember that the holy founder had two ways of instructing his religious. Sometimes it was in the parlor, during familiar conversations in which each one could pose questions, ask for solutions to her difficulties and seek enlightenment for her doubts.

Other times it was in the chapel of the monastery, before a restricted audience. Among these latter instructions one must make a further distinction. Some were given for solemnities in which the audience was relatively large. They reveal a very careful preparation and reveal clear and methodical divisions. Among these are found expositions of the highest mysteries of our Faith, such as the Trinity, the Incarnation, Redemption, etc. Often the holy bishop cites the inspired Books, works of the Fathers and Doctors of the Church, and develops these citations with the smoothness, the grace and the depth with which we are familiar in him.

He proceeds in another way when, without entirely excluding others, he addresses principally his religious. It is especially in the ceremonies for clothing and profession, when the holy founder embraces some chosen soul in order to "present her to Christ as a chaste virgin," that he finds in his heart the most tender, the most moving accents. His style becomes simpler and more imaginative, all the while maintaining a grave, even at times austere, hue. And this is something remarkable: These addresses, in which one might fear a certain sameness, assume a great variety of forms. It seems that everything presents this admirable orator with the opportunity of making delightful metaphors, and of drawing practical applications which are as ingenious as they are unexpected. Ordinarily he takes inspiration from the Gospel of the day or from the life of the saint whose feast it is; frequently, too, monastic practices and circumstances which are insignificant in themselves furnish material for allusions in which a perfect grace and dignity do not preclude a delicate irony whose point is completely softened by gentleness and charity.

In these familiar instructions the Bishop of Geneva eminently justifies the title of *Evangelium loquens* ("a Speaking Gospel") which his friend St. Vincent de Paul gives him. He ceaselessly preaches renunciation of self, humility, obedience, the renunciation of all covetousness—in a word, the death of the "old man," an indispensable condition for the incorporation of people into Our Lord Jesus Christ. The holy founder does not lose sight of the fact that the Visitation is "founded spiritually on Calvary." By preference he applies himself to riveting the sights of his daughters to this redeeming mountain; and if from time to time he permits them to contemplate the radiant heights of Tabor, it is only to remind them that the hour has not yet come for pitching a tent there as long as, remaining in the bonds of the flesh, "we journey far from the Lord."

One might find it surprising that, while addressing contemplatives, the saint speaks so little to them of prayer.

There are only four sermons which deal exclusively with this fundamental subject. But one must not forget that he often deals with this question in his *Spiritual Conferences* and that, further, the *Treatise on the Love of God* gives a direction to this holy exercise which is as complete as it is profound.

The sermons which make up this volume and the following were preserved almost entirely by the two religious to whom we are already indebted for the *Conferences:* Sisters Claude-Agnès Joly de La Roche and Marie-Marguerite Michel. Happily, both were gifted with an exceptional memory; they reproduced with a remarkable fidelity the teachings of their blessed Father. Nevertheless, each left in her version so unique a personal touch that it is easy to distinguish which is to be attributed to whom. Sister Claude-Agnès' style is flowing and rapid; this choice soul is easily at home among the most sublime subjects and clearly renders theological topics and argumentation which are at times a bit difficult. She knows how, at the right moment, to put aside details of secondary interest in order to throw into relief the major lines of the sermon.

Sister Marie-Marguerite's version presents a totally different character. Practical applications and homely anecdotes are reproduced with more fidelity. But, in contrast, her pen is easily at a loss with matters which are somewhat abstract. Her heavy and prolix sentences lack clarity and precision and are not always irreproachably correct.

The verification of this difference in style has been a major help to the editors in determining the probable date of a certain number of these sermons. Following the style of the redaction, they are divided into two characteristic groupings: Those which come from Sister Claude-Agnès de La Roche date from the first years of the Institute up to her departure for Orléans (from December, 1613 until July, 1620); those which Sister Marie-Marguerite Michel preserved for us date from August, 1620 until April, 1622. It is surprising that nothing has come down to us of the instructions which the holy founder most probably addressed to his daughters at Annecy during the summer and fall of 1622, the last year which he spent on earth. And this is not the only lack which we must admit. However rich our collection may be, it is certain that a large part of the sermons of St. Francis de Sales have not been collected, a fact established by contemporary documents. If good intentions were never lacking, often leisure time to record the sermons was, and the religious had to be content with preserving such teachings in their heart.

In addition to the sermons preached at Annecy, we possess several which were given by the holy founder in different monasteries of the Visitation: one at Bourges, five at Lyons, one at Belley. The tone is less familiar than in the others. One senses that the preacher is less at ease in addressing an audience where he is little known; but to judge by the scope of the collection, this audience was no less attentive than that at Annecy.

Value of the Sermons

The collected sermons are the continuation and development of the *Spiritual Conferences;* the same vigor is present in them and the same spirit inspires them. As always, the holy bishop here directs consequences back to their principle. If he earnestly recommends the practice of virtues, he insists more on the generating cause which brings them about. His great desire is to bring about the soul's true foundation and rootage in charity, so that from there it may, as if without effort, rise to all devotions and sacrifices. But this charity, as this Doctor of the Church shows it to us in its radiant furnace, is nothing other than the adorable Heart of Our Lord Jesus Christ. It seems that St. Francis de Sales is always trying to direct his hearers' attention toward, and to cause all their affection to converge upon, this unique Center of all holiness.

We have said it elsewhere, but one should not fail to mention again here that the glory of this holy founder is to have been one of the prophets of devotion to the Sacred Heart. He prepared the way for this beneficial devotion which ought to be the joy and hope of the Church in these times. As if he had a presentiment of the glorious mission destined for his Institute, he prepared it from afar to be worthy of it. [Dom Mackey is alluding to the role that the Visitandine nun, St. Margaret Mary, played in bringing about devotion to the Sacred Heart.] It is satisfying to state just how frequently in these sermons our delightful saint returns to this inexhaustible subject, and in terms which are as explicit as they are touching. Thus we will hear him assure us that the Savior "desires to give us" an abundance "of graces and blessings" and "even" His Heart; that His divine "side was opened" so that one could see the thoughts of His Heart which are thoughts "of pure and tender love"; and that "if we touch His Heart we will find it completely enflamed and burning with an incomparable love toward us."

Although similar passages could be cited here, it is better to permit the reader the pleasure of noticing them himself. Assuredly the reader will make his own this practical conclusion which will be the most beautiful fruit of devotion to the Sacred Heart: One needs "to have no other heart than that of God's, no other spirit than His, no other will than His, no other affections than His, nor any other desires than His—in short, we must be completely His."

—Dom B. Mackey, O.S.B.

— 1 —

THE GOAL OF PRAYER

Sermon for the Third Sunday of Lent, given on March 22, 1615, concerning the usefulness and necessity of prayer, the operations of the understanding, meditation, petitions, contemplation, and the goal of prayer.

St. Bernard—whose memory is dear to those who have to speak on prayer—in writing to a bishop, advised him that all that was necessary for him was to speak well (meaning to instruct, to discourse); then to do well in giving good example; and finally, to devote himself to prayer. And we, addressing this to all Christians, shall dwell upon the third point, which is prayer.

First, let us remark in passing that, although we condemn certain heretics of our time who hold that prayer is useless, we nevertheless do not hold with other heretics that it alone suffices for our justification. We say simply that it is so useful and necessary that without it we could not come to any good, seeing that by means of prayer we are shown how to perform all our actions well.

I have therefore consented to the desire which urges me to speak of prayer, even though it is not my intention to explain every aspect of it because we learn it more by experience than by being taught. Moreover, it matters little to know the kind of prayer. Actually, I would prefer that you never ask the name or the kind of prayer you are experiencing because, as St. Antony says, that prayer is imperfect in which one is aware that one is praying. Also,

1

prayer which one makes without knowing how one is doing it, and without reflecting on what one is asking for, shows clearly that such a soul is very much occupied with God and that, consequently, this prayer is excellent.

We shall treat, then, on the following four Sundays, of the final cause of prayer; of its efficient cause; of that which properly should not be called the "material cause," but rather the "object" of prayer; and of the effective cause of prayer itself. For now, I shall speak only of its final cause. But before entering upon the subject of prayer, I must say three or four little things that it is well to know.

Four operations pertain to our understanding: simple thought, study, meditation, and contemplation. Simple thought occurs when we go running over a great number of things, without any aim, as do flies that rest upon flowers, not seeking to extract any juice from them, but resting there only because they happen upon them. So it is with our understanding, passing from one thought to another. Even if these thoughts be of God, if they have no aim, far from being profitable, they are useless and detrimental and are a great obstacle to prayer.

Another operation of our understanding is study, and this takes place when we consider things only to know them, to understand them thoroughly or to be able to speak correctly of them, without having any other object than to fill our memory. In this we resemble beetles which settle upon the roses for no other end than to fill their stomachs and satiate themselves. Now, of these two operations of our understanding we shall speak no more, because they are not to our purpose.

Let us come to meditation. To know what meditation is, it is necessary to understand the words of King Hezekiah when the sentence of death was pronounced upon him, which was afterward revoked on account of his repentance. "I utter shrill cries," he said, "like a swallow," and "I moan like a dove,"[1] in the height of my sorrow. [Cf. *Is.* 38:14]. He meant to say: When the young swallow is all alone and its mother has gone in search of the herb called "celandine" in order to help it recover its sight, it cries, it pips, since it does not feel its mother near and because it does not see at all. So I, having lost my mother, which is grace, and seeing no one come to my aid, "I utter shrill cries." But he adds, "I moan like a dove." We must know that all birds are accustomed to open their beaks when they sing or chirp, except the dove, who makes her little song or cooing sound whilst holding her breath—and it is through the movement up and down which she makes of it, without letting it escape, that she produces her song. In like manner, meditation is made when we fix our understanding on a mystery from which we mean to draw good affections, for if we did not have this intention it would no longer be meditation, but study. Meditation is made, then, to move the affections, and particularly that of love. Indeed, meditation is the mother of the love of God and contemplation is the daughter of the love of God.

But between meditation and contemplation there is the petition which is made when, after having considered the goodness of Our Lord, His infinite love, His omnipotence, we become confident enough to ask for and entreat Him to give us what we desire. Now there are three kinds of petition, each of which is made differently: The first is made by justice, the second is made by authority, and the third is made by grace.

The petition which is made by justice cannot be called "prayer," although we use this word, because in a petition of justice we ask for a thing which is due to us. A petition which is made by authority ought not be called "prayer" either; for as soon as someone who has great authority over us—such as a parent, a lord or a master—uses the word "please,"[2] we say immediately to him, "You can command," or "Your 'please' serves as my command." But true prayer is that which is made by grace, i.e., when we ask for something which is not due to us at all, and when we ask it of someone who is far superior to us, as God is.

The fourth operation of our understanding is contemplation, which is nothing other than taking delight in the goodness of Him whom we have learned to know in meditation and whom we have learned to love by means of this knowledge. This delight will be our happiness in Heaven above.

We must now speak of the final cause [that is, the goal] of prayer. We ought to know in the first place that all things have been created for prayer, and that when God created angels and men, He did so that they might praise Him eternally in Heaven above, even though this is the last thing that we shall do—if that can be called "last" which is eternal. To understand this better we will say this: When we wish to make something we always look first to the end [or purpose], rather than to the work itself. For example, if we are to build a church and we are asked why we are building it, we will respond that it is so that we can retire there and sing the praises of God; nevertheless, this will be the last thing that we shall do. Another example: If you enter the apartment of a prince, you will see there an aviary of several little birds which are in a brightly colored and highly embellished cage. And if you want to know the end for which they have been placed there, it is to give pleasure to their master. If you look into another place, you will see there sparrow hawks, falcons and such birds of prey which have been hooded; these latter are for catching the partridge and other birds to delicately nourish the prince. But God, who is in no way carnivorous, does not keep birds of prey, but only the little birds which are enclosed in the aviary and destined to please Him. These little birds represent monks and nuns who have voluntarily enclosed themselves in monasteries that they may chant the praises of their God. So their principal exercise ought to be prayer and obedience to that saying which Our Lord gives in the Gospel: "Pray always." [*Lk.* 18:1].

The early Christians who had been trained by St. Mark the Evangelist were so assiduous in prayer that many of the ancient Fathers called them "suppliants," and others named them "physicians," because by means of prayer they found the remedy for all their ills. They also named them "monks," because they were so united; indeed, the name "monk" means "single." Pagan philosophers said that man is an uprooted tree, from which we can conclude how necessary prayer is for man, since if a tree does not have sufficient earth to cover its roots it cannot live; neither can a man live who does not give special attention to heavenly things. Now prayer, according to most of the Fathers, is nothing other than a raising of the mind to heavenly things; others say that it is a petition; but the two opinions are not at all opposed, for while raising our mind to God, we can ask Him for what seems necessary.

The principal petition which we ought to make to God is that of union of our wills with His, and the final cause of prayer lies in desiring only God. Accordingly, all perfection is contained therein, as Brother Giles, the companion of St. Francis [of Assisi], said when a certain person asked him what he could do in order to be perfect very soon. "Give," he replied, "one to One." That is to say, you have only one soul, and there is only one God; give your soul to Him and He will give Himself to you. The final cause of prayer, then, ought not to be to desire those tendernesses and consolations which Our Lord sometimes gives, since union does not consist in that, but rather in conforming to the will of God.

NOTES

1. The old French for "I moan" is "mediteray," which St. Francis de Sales is using as a pun for "meditate."
2. Francis de Sales is capitalizing on the fact that in the French language "please," "pray" and "prayer" are related.

— 2 —

THE SPIRIT OF PRAYER

Sermon for the Fourth Sunday of Lent, given on March 29, 1615, concerning who can pray, and the three conditions for praying well.

We have now to speak of the efficient cause of prayer. It is necessary for us to know, then, who can and who ought to pray. The question would soon be decided were we to say that all can pray and that all ought to do so. But in order the better to satisfy the mind, we shall treat this subject at greater length.

In the first place we must realize that God cannot pray at all, since prayer is a petition which is made by grace and requires that we know that we are in need of something, for we are not accustomed to ask for that which we already possess. Well, God can ask for nothing through grace, but rather, He does everything by divine authority. Moreover, He cannot have need of anything, since He possesses everything. It is therefore quite certain that God neither can nor ought to pray. So much for what regards God.

Many of the ancient Fathers, and also St. Gregory Nazianzen, teach that Our Lord Jesus Christ can no longer pray (as, being God, it is quite evident, since He is one same God with His Father; we have already spoken of this). They base their opinion on what this Divine Savior says to His disciples: I am going to My Father, but I do not say that I shall pray [Cf. *Jn.* 16:16,26]; and they add: If He does not say that He is going to pray, why should we say it? The rest of the Fathers hold that Our Lord does pray, because His well-beloved Apostle wrote, speaking of his Master, that we have an intercessor in the presence of the Father. [Cf. *1 Jn.* 2:1].

Nevertheless, they do not contradict each other by their different opinions, although it may seem so. For it is certain that Our Lord Jesus Christ does not *have* to pray, but can *by justice* ask of His Father what He wishes. We see, too, that advocates are not accustomed to ask as favors, but rather they ask according to justice, for the rights which they uphold. It is indeed on sure grounds that the Savior asks, for He shows His wounds to His Father when He desires to obtain something. Nevertheless, it is a most certain truth that although Our Lord asks by justice for what He wants, He does not cease, as man, to humble Himself before His Father, speaking to Him with a deep reverence and making more profound acts of humility than ever any creature either knew how to or could make; in this sense His petition can be called "prayer."

We find in some passages of Scripture that the Holy Spirit has petitioned and prayed. [Cf. *Rom.* 8:26-27]. From this it ought not to be understood that He is actually praying, for being equal to the Father and to the Son He cannot pray; but it means that He has inspired man to make such a prayer.

The angels pray, and this has been shown to us in several passages of Holy Scripture. [Cf. *Tob.* 12; *Rev.* 8:3-4]. But for people who are in Heaven we have not so much testimony, because before Our Lord died, rose and ascended into Heaven there were no people at all in Paradise; they were all in Abraham's bosom. Nevertheless, it is quite evident that the saints and the people who are in Paradise do pray, since they are with the angels who pray.

Let us see now if all people can pray. I say yes, and that no one can excuse himself from doing so, not even heretics. Moreover, there was once a pagan [Cf. *Acts* 10:4, 30-31] who made a prayer which was so excellent that it deserved to be presented before the throne of the Divine Majesty;

and God granted him the grace of the means of being instructed in the Faith, and afterward he was a great saint among the Christians.

It is true that great sinners experience great difficulty in praying. They resemble very young birds who, as soon as they have their feathers, are able to fly by themselves by means of their wings; but if they happen to perch upon birdlime which has been prepared to catch them, who does not see that this sticky substance will adhere to their wings so that afterward they will be unable to fly? Thus it happens to sinners—who so entangle themselves and settle into the sticky substance of vice, and so allow themselves to be stuck to sin, that they cannot soar to Heaven by prayer. Nevertheless, so long as they are capable of grace, they are also capable of prayer. It is only the devil who is incapable of prayer, because he alone is incapable of love.

All that remains is for us to state the necessary conditions to pray well. I know indeed that the ancients who treat this matter cite a great many such conditions; some count 15, others eight. But since this number is so large, I limit myself to mentioning only three. The first is that one be little by humility; the second, that one be great in hope; and the third, that one be grafted onto Jesus Christ crucified.

Let us speak of the first, which is nothing other than that spiritual mendicancy of which Our Lord says: Blessed are the mendicant in spirit, for theirs is the Kingdom of Heaven. [Cf. *Mt.* 5:3]. And although some of the Doctors interpret these words thus: How happy are the poor in spirit, these two interpretations are not opposed, because all the poor are mendicants [beggars] if they are not proud, and all mendicants are poor if they are not avaricious. In order to pray well, then, we must acknowledge that we are poor, and we must greatly humble ourselves; for do you not see how a marksman with a crossbow, when he wishes to discharge a large arrow, draws the string of his bow lower the higher he wants it to go? Thus must we do when we wish our prayer to reach Heaven; we must lower ourselves by the awareness of our nothingness. David admonishes us to do so by these words: When you wish to pray, plunge yourself profoundly into the abyss of your nothingness that you may be able afterward, without difficulty, to let your prayer fly like an arrow even up to the heavens. [Cf. *Ps.* 130:1-2; *Sir.* 35:21].

Do you not see that nobles who wish to make water rise to the top of their castles go to the source of this water in some highly elevated place and then convey it by pipes, forcing it to descend for as great a distance as they wish it to rise? Otherwise the water would never rise. And if you ask them how they made it rise, they will answer you that it rises through this descent. It is the same with prayer; for if you ask how it is that prayer can rise to Heaven, you will be told that it rises there through the descent of humility. The spouse in the Song of Songs[1] astonishes the angels and makes them say: Who is this who comes from the desert, and who rises like a column of smoke, laden with myrrh and frankincense and with every perfume known, and who is leaning upon her Lover? [Cf. *Song* 3:6; 8:5]. Humility in its beginning is a desert, although in the end it may be very fruitful, and the soul that is humble thinks itself as being in a desert where neither birds nor even savage beasts dwell, and where there is no fruit tree at all.

Let us pass on now to hope, which is the second necessary condition for praying well. The spouse coming up from the desert rises like a shoot or column of smoke, laden with myrrh. This represents hope, for even though myrrh gives off a pleasant odor, it is nevertheless bitter to the taste. Likewise, hope is pleasant since it promises that we shall one day possess what we long for, but it is bitter because we are not now enjoying what we love. Incense is far more appropriate as the symbol of hope, because, being placed upon fire, it always sends its smoke upward; likewise, it is necessary that hope be placed upon charity, otherwise it would no longer be hope, but rather presumption. Hope, like an arrow, darts up even to the gate of Heaven, but it cannot enter there because it is a virtue wholly of earth. If we want our prayer to penetrate Heaven we must whet the arrow with the grindstone of love.

Let us come to the third necessary condition. The angels say that the spouse is leaning upon her Lover; we have seen that for the last condition it is necessary to be grafted onto Jesus Christ crucified. The [Divine] Spouse praised His spouse, saying that she was like a lily among thorns. She, in turn, answered Him: My Lover is like an apple tree among the trees of the woods; this tree is completely laden with leaves, flowers and fruit; I shall rest in its shadow and receive the fruit which falls into my lap and eat it, and having chewed it, I shall relish it in my mouth, where I shall find it sweet and agreeable. [Cf. *Song* 2:2-3]. But where is this tree planted? In what woods will we find it? Without doubt it is planted on Mount Calvary, and we must keep ourselves in its shadow. But what are its leaves? They are nothing other than the hope that we have of our salvation by means of the death of the Savior. And its flowers? They are the prayers that He offered up to His Father for us [Cf. *Heb.* 5:7]; the fruits are the merits of His Passion and Death.

Let us remain then at the foot of this Cross, and let us never depart from there, so that we may be all saturated with the Blood which flows from it. St. Catherine of Siena once had an ecstasy while meditating on the Passion and Death of Our Lord. It seemed to her that she was in a bath of His Precious Blood, and when she came to herself she saw her dress all red with this Blood, but others did not see it. We, too, must never go to prayer without being similarly bathed; at least it is necessary to be thus bathed in the morning at our first prayer. St. Paul, writing to his dear children [Cf. *Rom.* 13:14], told them to be clothed with Our Lord, that is to say, with His Blood.

But what is it to be clothed with this Blood? Do you not

know that we say: There is a man clothed in scarlet; and scarlet is a fish. That garment is made of wool, but it is dyed in the blood of the fish. [Cf. *Oeuvres,* vol. VIII, p. 144]. In like manner, even though we are clothed with wool, by which it is understood that we perform good works, these good works—though from us—have neither worth nor value if they are not dyed in the Blood of our Master, whose merits render them agreeable to the Divine Majesty.

When Jacob wished to obtain his father Isaac's blessing, his mother made him prepare a kid in venison sauce because Isaac liked it. [Cf. *Gen.* 27: 9-29]. She also made him wear the skins of the kid on his hands, because Esau, the elder son to whom the blessing belonged by right, was all hairy. She even made Jacob wear the scented garment destined for the eldest son of the home. She led him thus to her husband, who was blind. When Jacob asked for the blessing, Isaac felt his hands and cried aloud: Ah, but I am in such pain! The voice I hear is that of my son Jacob, but the hands I feel are those of Esau. And having smelled the scented garment, he said: The good fragrance that I have savored has given me such delight that I give my blessing to my son. So too we, having prepared this spotless Lamb [Cf. *1 Pet.* 1:19] and having presented Him to the Eternal Father to satisfy His taste, when we ask for His blessing He will say, if we are clothed with the Blood of Jesus Christ: The voice that I hear is Jacob's, but the hands (which are our evil deeds) are those of Esau; nevertheless, because of the delight with which I savor the fragrance of his garment, I give him My blessing. Amen.

NOTES

1. The book of the Bible known as the "Song of Songs" (also called the "Canticle of Canticles" or "Song of Solomon") describes in symbolic language the happy union between Christ and His spouse. The Divine Spouse (the Lover, or Bridegroom) is Christ; Christ's spouse (the bride) is the Church, and most particularly the happiest part of the Church, that is, perfect souls, every one of which is His beloved; but above all others, the spouse is the Immaculate Virgin Mary.

3

THE KINDS OF PRAYER

Sermon for Passion Sunday, given on April 5, 1615, concerning the prayers of sinners, what to ask God for, vital prayer, vocal prayer, obligatory and non-obligatory prayers, and the Divine Office.

We have shown that the end of prayer is our union with God, and that all who are on the way to salvation can and ought to pray. But there remained to us a difficulty in our last exhortation, namely, whether sinners can be heard. For do you not see that the man born blind who is mentioned in the Gospel [Cf. *Jn.* 9:31], and whose sight Our Lord restored, said to those who questioned him that God does not hear sinners? But let him say it, for he was still speaking as a blind man.

We must realize that there are three kinds of sinners: impenitent sinners, penitent sinners, and justified sinners. Now, it is an assured fact that impenitent sinners are not heard at all, seeing that they wish to wallow in their sins; moreover, their prayers are an abomination before God. He Himself made this clear to those who said to him: Why do we fast and afflict ourselves and You take no note of it? [Cf. *Is.* 58:3]. Answering them, God said: Your fasts, your mortifications, and your festivals are an abomination to Me, since in the midst of all these things your hands are stained with blood. [Cf. *Is.* 58:3-5; 1:13-15; 59:3]. The prayer of such sinners cannot be good, because "no one can say: 'Jesus is Lord,' except in the Holy Spirit" [1 *Cor.*

12:3], and no one can call God "Father" unless he has been adopted as His son. [Cf. *Rom.* 8:15; *Gal.* 4:5-6]. The sinner who wishes to remain in his sin is unable to pronounce the sovereign name of Our Lord because he does not have the Holy Spirit with him, for the Holy Spirit does not dwell in a heart stained with sin. [Cf. *Wis.* 1:4-5]. Do you not know, moreover, that no one comes to the Father but in virtue of His Son's name, since He Himself has said that whatever we ask His Father in His Name we shall obtain? [Cf. *Jn.* 14:6, 13; 16:23]. The prayers of the impenitent sinner, then, are not agreeable to God at all.

Let us come to the penitent sinner. Without doubt we are wrong to call him a sinner, for he is no longer so, since he already detests his sin. And if indeed the Holy Spirit is not yet in his heart by residence, He is there nevertheless by assistance. For who do you think gives him this repentance for having offended God if not the Holy Spirit, since we would not know how to have a good thought toward our salvation if He did not give it to us? [Cf. 2 *Cor.* 3:5]. But has this poor man not done anything on his part? Yes, most certainly he has. Listen to the words of David: Lord, You looked upon me when I was in the quagmire of my sin. You opened my heart and I did not close it. You have drawn me and I have not let go. You have urged me and I have not turned back. [Cf. *Ps.* 102:18, 20-21; 103:3-4 and *Is.* 50:5]. We have plenty of proof that prayers of penitent sinners are agreeable to the Divine Majesty. But I shall content myself with citing the example of the publican who went up to the Temple a sinner and came down from it justified, thanks to the humble prayer he had made. [Cf. *Lk.* 18:10-14].

Let us go on now to the "matter" of prayer. I shall say nothing of its end, for I shall speak of that next Sunday. The matter of prayer is to ask of God all that is good. But we must understand that there are two kinds of goods, spiritual goods and temporal or corporal goods. In the Song of Songs, the spouse praised her Well-Beloved, saying that

His lips were lilies which drip choice myrrh [Cf. *Song* 5:13], to which her [Divine] Spouse replied that she had honey and milk under her tongue. [Cf. *Song* 4:11].

I know indeed that these words are interpreted in this sense, namely, that when preaching to the people, preachers have honey under their tongue, and when speaking to God in prayer on behalf of the people, they have milk under their tongue. According to a second interpretation, preachers have milk under their tongue when preaching on the virtues of Our Lord as Man: His gentleness, mildness and mercy; and they have honey under their tongue when speaking of His Divinity. There are many who are mistaken in thinking that honey is made only from the juice of flowers. Honey is a liquor which falls from the heavens amidst the dew. In falling upon flowers, it takes their flavor, as do all liquors which are put into vessels which contain any kind of flavor. Honey thus represents the divine perfections, which are entirely celestial.

Let us apply these words of the [Divine] Spouse to our prayer. We have said that there are two kinds of goods which we may ask for in prayer: spiritual goods and corporal goods. There are two kinds of spiritual goods. One kind is necessary for our salvation; these we ought to ask God for simply and without condition, for He wants to give them to us. The other kind, although spiritual, we ought to ask for under the same conditions as corporal goods, that is, if it is God's will and if it is for His greater glory; with these conditions we may ask for anything.

Now the spiritual goods which are necessary for our salvation, signified by the honey which the spouse has under her tongue, are faith, hope and charity, as well as the other virtues which lead to them. The other spiritual goods are ecstasies, raptures, spiritual comforts and consolations, none of which ought we to ask of God except conditionally, because they are not at all necessary for our salvation.

There are those who think that if they were gifted with

wisdom they would be much more capable of loving God, but that is simply not so. You will remember, indeed, that Brother Giles once went to St. Bonaventure and said to him: Oh, how happy you are, my Father, to be so learned, for you can love God far better than we who are ignorant. Then St. Bonaventure told him that knowledge did not help him at all in loving God, and that a simple woman was capable of loving Him as much as the most learned man in the world.

But who does not see the delusion of those who are always after their spiritual Father in order to complain that they experience none of these tender feelings and consolations in their prayers? Do you not see that if you had them you would not be able to escape vainglory, nor would you be able to prevent your self-love from being pleased with itself because of them, so that you would end in amusing yourself more with the gifts than with the Giver? Thus it is a great mercy to you that God does not give you them at all. And you must not lose courage on that account, since perfection does not consist in having these spiritual consolations and affections, but in having our will united to that of God. It is this that we may and ought to ask from the Divine Majesty unconditionally.

Tobit, being already old and wishing to set his affairs in order, commanded his son to go to Rages to get a sum of money which was owed him. For this purpose he gave him a signed document with which the money could not be refused him. [Cf. *Tob.* 4:21-22; 5:3-4]. We must do likewise when we wish to ask of the Eternal Father His Paradise, or an increase of our faith, or of His love—all of which He wishes to grant us, provided we bring His Son's signed document, that is to say, provided that we always ask in the Name and through the merits of Our Lord.

This good Master has shown us very clearly the order that we must follow in our petitions, enjoining us to pray to the Father, "Hallowed be Thy Name, Thy Kingdom come, Thy will be done." We ought accordingly to ask first that

His Name be hallowed, that is to say, that He may be acknowledged and adored by all; after which we ask what is most necessary for us, namely, that His Kingdom come for us, so that we may be inhabitants of Heaven; and then, that His will be done. And after these three requests we add, "Give us this day our daily bread." Jesus Christ makes us say, "Give us our daily bread," because under this word "bread" are included all temporal goods.

We ought to be very moderate in asking for these goods here below and we should fear much in asking for them, because we do not know whether Our Lord will give them to us at all in His anger. This is why those who pray with perfection ask for very few of these goods, remaining rather before God like children before their father, placing in Him all their confidence—or indeed, like a valet who serves his master well, for he does not go every day and ask for his food, knowing that his services claim it well enough for him. So much for the "matter" of prayer.

The ancient Fathers note that there are three kinds of prayer, namely, vital prayer, mental prayer, and vocal prayer. We shall not now speak of mental prayer, but only of vital prayer and vocal prayer. Every action of those who live in the fear of God is a continual prayer, and this is called "vital prayer." It is said that St. John [the Baptist], while in the desert, lived on locusts [Cf. *Matt.* 3:4] or grasshoppers, and cicadas, that he ate no grapes, nor drank ale or anything which could intoxicate. [Cf. *Lk.* 1:15]. I shall not dwell on all that, but only on the fact that he ate nothing but locusts, or grasshoppers.

No one knows whether locusts are of Heaven or of earth for they dart continually toward Heaven, but they also fall to the earth sometimes. They are nourished by the dew which falls from Heaven and they are always singing, and what is heard is nothing other than a reverberation or twittering which is made in their breasts. With good reason did the blessed St. John nourish himself with grasshoppers, since he was himself a mystical grasshopper. No one knows whether he was of Heaven or of earth, for although he sometimes touched earth in order to attend to his needs, he rose up suddenly and darted heavenward, nourished more by heavenly than by earthly meats. Do you not see his great abstinence? He ate only locusts and drank only water, and then only moderately. He also sang the praises of God almost continually, for he himself was a voice. [Cf. *Jn.* 1:23]. In short, his life was a continual prayer. Likewise we may say that those who give alms, who visit the sick, and who practice all such good works, are praying, and these same good actions call to God for a reward.

Let us go on now to vocal prayer. To mutter something with the lips is not praying if one's heart is not joined to it. To speak, it is necessary first to have conceived interiorly what we wish to say. There is first the interior word, and then the spoken word, which causes what the interior has first pronounced to be understood. Prayer is nothing other than speaking to God. Now it is certain that to speak to God without being attentive to Him and to what we say to Him is something that is most displeasing to Him.

A holy person relates that a parrot or popinjay was taught to recite the *Ave Maria.* This bird once flew off, and a sparrow hawk pounced upon it; but when the parrot began repeating the *Ave Maria,* the sparrow hawk let it go. It is not that Our Lord listened to the prayer of the parrot; no, for it is an unclean bird [Cf. *Lev.* 11:19], which was therefore unfit to be offered in sacrifice. Nevertheless, He permitted this to show how pleasing this prayer is to Him. Prayers of those who pray like this parrot are loathsome to God, for He tests more the heart of him who prays than the words which he pronounces. [Cf. *Is.* 1:13 and *Prov.* 24:12].

It is necessary for us to know that vocal prayer is of three kinds: Some are commanded, others recommended, and still others are completely optional. Those which are commanded are the Our Father and the Creed, which we ought to recite every day, something which Our Lord made very clear when He said, "Give us this day our daily bread." This shows us that we must ask for it every day. And if you tell me that you have never prayed daily, I shall answer you that you resemble beasts. The other prayer which is commanded for those of us who are of the Church is the Office,[1] and if we omit any considerable part of it, we sin. Those which are only recommended are the Our Fathers or rosaries which are prescribed for the gaining of indulgences. If we omit saying these, we do not sin, but our good Mother the Church, to show us that she wishes us to say them, grants indulgences to those who do recite them. Optional prayers are all those which we say other than those of which we have just spoken.

Although the prayers that we say voluntarily may be very good, those recommended are much better because the holy virtue of compliance comes into play in praying them. It is as if we were to say: You desire, my good Mother the Church, that I do this, and though you do not command me to do so, I am very glad to do it to please you. There is already a little of obedience in this. But the prayers which are commanded have a different value altogether on account of the obedience attached to them, and without doubt there is also more charity in them.

Now among these, some are community prayers and others are private. Community prayers are Mass, the Office, and prayers which are recited in times of calamities. O God, with how much reverence ought we to assist at these services, but prepared quite differently than for private prayers, because in the latter we treat only of our own affairs before God, or if we pray for the Church, we do so in charity. But in community prayers we pray for all in general. St. Augustine relates that once while he was still a pagan he entered a church where St. Ambrose was having the Office chanted alternately [by two choirs], as it has been done since then. He was so enraptured and ecstatic that he thought he was in Paradise. Many persons assert that they have oftentimes seen troupe after troupe of angels coming to assist at the Divine Office. With what attention then ought we not to assist at it, seeing that the angels are present and repeat on high in the Church triumphant what we are saying here below!

But perhaps we will say that if we had seen the angels at our Office, we would bring more attention and reverence to it. Ah, no, pardon me, but there would certainly be nothing of the kind. For even if we had been snatched up with St. Paul to the third Heaven [Cf. 2 *Cor.* 12:2], even if we had dwelt 30 years in Paradise, if we were not rooted in faith, all that would mean nothing. I have often pondered over the fact that St. Peter, St. James and St. John, even after having seen Our Lord in His Transfiguration, did not fail to desert Him in His Passion and Death.

We ought never to come to the Office, especially we who chant it, without making an act of contrition and asking the assistance of the Holy Spirit before beginning it. Oh, how happy are we to begin here below what we shall do eternally in Heaven, where the Father, the Son and the Holy Spirit lead us. Amen.

NOTES

1. St. Francis de Sales is referring to the obligation of all priests and of some members of religious orders to pray the Divine Office daily. The Mass and the Divine Office constitute the official prayer of the Church.

4

THE HEART OF PRAYER

Sermon for Palm Sunday, given on April 12, 1615, concerning direct and indirect prayer, bodily posture during prayer, the four levels of the soul, meditation, contemplation, and ejaculations.

I still have to point out the distinction that exists in prayer, whether mental or vocal prayer. In prayer we go to God in two ways, both of which have been recommended to us by Our Lord and commanded by our Holy Mother the Church—namely, sometimes we pray directly to God, and at other times indirectly, as when we say the anthems of Our Lady, the *Salve Regina* and others. When we pray directly we exercise the filial confidence which is founded upon faith, hope and charity; when we pray indirectly and through the intercession of another, we practice the holy humility which springs from self-knowledge. When we go directly to God we proclaim His goodness and mercy, in which we place all our confidence; but when we pray indirectly, that is, when we implore the assistance of Our Lady, of the saints and of the blessed, it is so that we might better be received by the Divine Majesty, and then we proclaim His greatness and omnipotence, and the reverence which we owe Him.

I should like to add another word to the remarks I made the other day on the exterior reverence which we ought to have when we pray. Our Mother the Church indicates all the postures she wishes us to assume in reciting the Office:

Sometimes she will have us standing, sometimes sitting, then kneeling; sometimes with the head covered, sometimes uncovered; but all these positions and postures are nothing other than prayers. All the ceremonies of the Church are full of very great mysteries, and humble, simple, devout people find the greatest consolation in assisting at them. What do you think that the palms which we carry in our hands today signify? Nothing other than our asking God that He render us victorious by the merits of the victory which Our Lord won for us on the tree of the cross.

When we are at the Office we must be careful to observe the postures prescribed for us by the rubrics; but in our private prayers, what reverence ought we to have? In private prayer, we are before God as in public prayer, although in public prayer we ought to be particularly attentive on account of the edification of our neighbor; exterior reverence is a great aid to the interior. We have many examples which witness to the great exterior reverence which we ought to have when praying, even though it be private prayer. Listen to St. Paul: I kneel, he says, before the Father of Our Lord Jesus Christ for you all. [Cf. *Eph.* 3:14]. And don't you see that the Savior Himself, while praying to His Father, is prostrate to the ground? [Cf. *Mt.* 26:39 and *Mk.* 14:35].

Here is one more example. I think you know that the great hermit St. Paul lived for many years in the desert. St. Antony [of the Desert], having gone to see him, found him in prayer. After speaking with him, St. Antony left him. But having come a second time to visit him, he found St. Paul in the same position as before, his head raised and his eyes fixed on Heaven, kneeling upright, with hands joined. St. Antony, having already waited for him a long time, began to wonder, because he did not hear him sigh as usual; he then raised his eyes and looked into his face and found that he was dead. It seems that St. Paul's body, which had prayed so much during life, continued to pray after his death. In short, it is necessary that the whole person pray.

David says that his whole face prayed [Cf. *Ps.* 27:8], that his eyes were so attentive in looking upon God that they failed [Cf. *Ps.* 69:4 and 88:10; also *Is.* 38:14], and that his mouth was open like a little bird who waits for its mother to come to fill it. But in any case, the posture which affords the best attention is the most suitable. Yes, even the posture of lying down is good, and seems to be a prayer in itself. For do you not see that the holy man Job, lying on his dunghill, made a prayer so excellent that it merited to be heard by God? [Cf. *Job* 42:9-10]. But this is sufficient.

Let us now speak of mental prayer; and if it pleases you, I shall show you, through a comparison with the Temple of Solomon, how there are four levels in the soul. [Cf. St. Francis de Sales: *Treatise on the Love of God,* Bk. 1, ch. 12]. In that Temple there was first a court which was set aside for the Gentiles, so that no one might be able to ex- cuse himself from divine worship. It was because there was no nation which could not come to render praise in that place that this Temple was so pleasing to the Divine Ma- jesty. The second court was destined for the Jews, both men and women, though later a separation was made in order to avoid the scandals which might arise in such a mixed assembly. Then, mounting higher, there was another place for the priests, and finally there was a court destined for the cherubim and their Master, where the Ark of the Covenant rested and where God manifested His will, and this place was called the *Sancta Sanctorum* [that is, the Holy of Holies].

In our souls there is the first level, which is a certain knowledge that we have through our senses, as by our eyes we know that such an object is green, red or yellow. But after this there is a degree or level which is still a little higher, namely, a knowledge that we have by means of consideration. For example, a man who has been ill-treated in a certain place will consider what he will be able to do in order not to return there. The third level is the knowledge we have through faith. The fourth, the *Sancta Sanctorum,* is the highest point of our soul, which we call spirit, and so long as this highest point is always fixed on God, we need not be troubled in the least.

Ships at sea all have a mariner's needle, which always points to the north star, and though the boat may be heading southward, the needle nevertheless does not fail to point always north. Thus it sometimes seems that the soul is going straight for the south, so greatly is it agitated by distractions; nevertheless, the highest point of the spirit always looks toward its God, who is its north. Sometimes people who are the most advanced have such great temptations, even against faith, that it seems to them that their whole soul consents, so greatly is it disturbed. They have only this highest point which resists, and it is this part of ourselves which makes mental prayer, for although all our other faculties and powers may be filled with distractions, the spirit, its fine point, is praying.

Now in mental prayer there are four parts, the first of which is meditation; the second, contemplation; the third, ejaculations; and the fourth, a simple attention to the presence of God. The first is made by way of meditation, in this manner: We take a mystery, for instance Our Lord crucified. Then having pictured Him to ourselves thus, we consider His virtues: the love which He bore to His Father, which made Him suffer death, even death on a cross [Cf. *Phil.* 2:8], rather than displease Him, or to speak better, in order to please Him; the great gentleness, humility and patience with which He suffered so many injuries; and finally, His immense charity toward those who put Him to death, praying for them amidst His most excruciating sufferings. [Cf. *Lk.* 23:34]. Having considered all these points, our affections will be moved with an ardent desire to imitate Him in His virtues; we will then implore the Eternal Father to render us true images of His Son. [Cf. *Rom.* 8:29].

Meditation is made as the bees make and gather honey:

They go out gathering the honey which falls from heaven upon the flowers, and extract a little of the juice from the same flower, and then carry it into their hives. Thus, we go along picking out the virtues of Our Lord one after the other in order to draw from them the desire of imitation. (Afterward, we consider them collectively at a single glance by contemplation.) At the creation, God meditated [Cf. *Treatise,* Bk. 6, ch. 5], for do you not see that after He had created heaven He said that it was good? And He did the same after He had created the earth, the animals, and then, finally man. He found everything good, considering it one at a time, but seeing all together that which He had made, He said that it was *very* good. [Cf. *Gen.* 1:10-25, 31].

The spouse in the Song of Songs, having praised her [Divine] Beloved for the beauty of His eyes, His lips, in short, of all His members one after another [Cf. *Song* 5:9-16], concluded in this way: O, how beautiful is my Beloved; oh, how I love Him, He is my very dear one! This is contemplation, for by dint of considering in mystery after mystery how good God is, we become like the ropes of our barges. When we row very hard these ropes so heat up that if we were not to wet them they would catch fire; but our soul, growing warm from loving Him whom it has found so lovable, continues to gaze upon Him because it delights more and more in beholding Him, so beautiful and so good.

The [Divine] Spouse in the Song of Songs says: Come, my beloved, for I have gathered My myrrh, I have eaten My bread and My honeycomb with its honey, I have drunk My wine with My milk. Come, My beloved ones, and eat; be inebriated, My dearest ones. [Cf. *Song* 5:1, according to the *Septuagint* and the Fathers; also *Treatise,* Bk. 6, ch. 6]. These words represent for us the mysteries we are about to celebrate in these following weeks. "I have gathered My myrrh, I have eaten My bread": this was in the Passion and Death of the Savior. "I have eaten My honey with My honeycomb": this was when He reunited His soul with His

body. Finally the Spouse adds, "My wine with My milk."
The wine represents the joy of His Resurrection, and the
milk, the sweetness of His conversation. He drank them
together, for He dwelt on earth for 40 days after His
Resurrection [Cf. *Acts* 1:3], visiting His disciples, making
them touch His wounds, and eating with them. Now when
He says, "Eat, My beloved ones," He means, "Meditate";
for do you not know that in order to render meat fit to be
swallowed it is necessary first to chew it and make it
smaller, and to toss it from side to side in the mouth? So
we must do with the mysteries of Our Lord: We must chew
them and turn them over several times in our mind, first to
warm our will and then to pass on to contemplation.

The Spouse concludes with the following: "Be inebriated,
My dearest ones." And what does He mean? You know
well that we are not wont to chew wine, but only to
swallow it; this represents to us contemplation in which we
no longer chew, but only swallow. "You have meditated
enough upon the fact that I am good," the Divine Spouse
seems to say to His beloved; "behold Me, and take delight
in *seeing* that I am so."

St. Francis [of Assisi] passed an entire night repeating:
You are "my All." Being in contemplation, he pronounced
these words, as if wishing to say: I have considered You
piece by piece, O My Lord, and I found that You are very
lovable; now I behold You and see that You are "my All."
St. Bruno was content to say, "O Goodness!" And St.
Augustine: "O Beauty ever ancient and ever new!" You are
ancient because You are eternal, but You are new because
You bring a new sweetness to my heart. These are words of
contemplation. [Cf. *Treatise* Bk. 6, ch. 5].

Let us proceed to the third part of mental prayer, which
is made by way of ejaculations. No one can be excused
from making this because it can be made while coming and
going about one's business. You tell me that you do not
have the time to give two or three hours to prayer; who
asks you to do so? Recommend yourself to God the first

thing in the morning, protest that you do not wish to offend Him, and then go about your affairs, resolved, nevertheless, to raise your spirit to God, even amidst company. Who can prevent you from speaking to Him in the depth of your heart, since it makes no difference whether you speak to Him mentally or vocally? Make short but fervent aspirations. The one which St. Francis repeated is excellent, although this was an aspiration of contemplation, because it continues like a river which is ever flowing. It is true that to say to God: You are "my All," and to desire something else other than Him, would not be right, because our words should conform to the sentiments of our heart. But we ought not to hesitate to say to God, "I love You," even if we do not have a strong feeling of love, since we wish to love Him and to have an ardent desire of doing so.

A good way to accustom ourselves to making these ejaculations is to take the petitions of the Our Father one after another, choosing a sentence for each day. For example, today you have taken "Our Father who art in Heaven"; thus, at first you will say, "My Father, You who are in Heaven"; and a quarter of an hour afterward you will say, "If You are my Father, when shall I be wholly Your daughter?" Thus you will go on continually after each quarter of an hour to another part of your prayer.

The holy Fathers who lived in the desert, those old and true religious, were so assiduous in making these prayers and ejaculations that St. Jerome relates that when someone went to visit them they heard one of the Fathers saying, "You, O my God, are all that I desire"; and another Father: "When shall I be all Yours, O my God"; and another repeating: "Deign, O God, to rescue me." [Cf. *Ps.* 70:2]. In short, they heard a most agreeable harmony in the variety of their voices. But you will say to me: If we say these words vocally, why do you call it mental prayer? Because it is made mentally also, and because it comes first from the heart.

The [Divine] Spouse says in the Song of Songs that His

beloved has ravished His heart with one glance of her eyes and by one of her hairs which falls upon her neck. [Cf. *Song* 4:9, according to the *Septuagint*]. These words are a quiver full of most agreeable and most delightful interpretations. Here is one which is very pleasing: When a husband and wife have affairs in their household which compel them to be separated, if it happens by chance that they meet, they glance at one another as they pass—but it is only, as it were, with one eye, because in meeting sideways, they cannot well do so with both. In like manner this Spouse wishes to say: Although My beloved may be very much occupied, nevertheless she does not fail to look at Me with one eye, assuring Me by this glance that she is all Mine. She has ravished My heart with one of her hairs which falls upon her neck, that is to say, with one thought which comes from her heart.

We shall not speak now of our fourth part of mental prayer. Oh, how happy we shall be if we ever reach Heaven; for there we shall meditate, looking at and considering all the works of God in detail, and we shall see that each of them is good; we shall contemplate, and shall see that all together they are *very* good, and we shall dart forth eternally in Him.[1]

It is there that I wish you to be. Amen.

NOTES

1. St. Francis de Sales is referring to the great joyful enthusiasm of the blessed in Heaven. (His words here are not easily translated into English.)

INDEX

Index to the Sermons on Prayer

Index to the Introductory Material

At your bookdealer or direct from the Publisher.

At your bookdealer or direct from the Publisher.

NOTES

NOTES

NOTES

NOTES